**Supporting Learning in Schools**

D0297605

 **Hampshire**
County Council

## What animals live here?

# POLAR LANDS

Mary-Jane Wilkins

**W**

## FRANKLIN WATTS
LONDON · SYDNEY

Franklin Watts
First published in Great Britain in 2016 by
The Watts Publishing Group

For Brown Bear Books Ltd:
Picture Researcher: Clare Newman
Designer: Melissa Roskell
Design Manager: Keith Davis
Editorial Director: Lindsey Lowe
Children's Publisher: Anne O'Daly

ISBN 978 1 4451 5173 1

Printed in China

Franklin Watts
An imprint of
Hachette Children's Group
Part of The Watts Publishing Group
Carmelite House
50 Victoria Embankment
London EC4Y 0DZ

An Hachette UK company
www.hachette.co.uk

www.franklinwatts.co.uk

**Picture Credits**
The photographs in this book are used by
permission and through the courtesy of:

Front Cover: Shutterstock: Anita Andre tl, BMJ cl,
Evgeny Kovalev main, Vladimir Melnik bl, Elena
Shchipkova br;
Inside: 1, ©Shutterstock/Bike Rider London; 4,
©Shutterstock/Armin Rose; 4-5, ©Shutterstock/
Elnavegante; 6, ©Shutterstock/Anita Andre; 6-7,
©Shutterstock/Florida Stock; 8, ©FLPA/Michio
Hosino/Minden Pictures; 9, ©Shutterstock/
BMJ; 10, ©FLPA/Samuel Blanc/Biosphoto;
10-11, ©Shutterstock/Volt Collection; 12,
©Shutterstock/Sylvie Bouchard; 12-13, © FLPA/T.
W. P./Imagebroker; 14, ©Shutterstock/Cedric
Weber; 14-15, ©FLPA/Hiroya Minakuchi/Minden
Pictures; 16, ©FLPA/Sergey Gorshkov/Minden
Pictures; 16-17, ©Shutterstock/Outdoorsman; 18,
©Thinkstock/Eva Pum/iStock; 19, ©Shutterstock/
Tony Brindley; 20, ©Shutterstock/Jeff McGraw;
20-21, ©Shutterstock/Sergey Krasnoshchokov;
22, ©Shutterstock/Volodymyr Goinyk; 23,
©Shutterstock/Mikhail Kolesnikov.
T=Top, C=Centre, B=Bottom, L=Left, R=Right

Brown Bear Books has made every attempt to
contact the copyright holder. If you have any
information please contact:
licensing@brownbearbooks.co.uk

# CONTENTS

Where are the polar lands? ............ 4

Polar bear ......................................... 6

Harp seal ......................................... 8

Walrus .............................................. 9

Emperor penguin ...........................10

Musk ox ..........................................12

Whales .............................................14

Arctic fox .........................................16

Lemming ..........................................18

Arctic tern ....................................... 19

Caribou ........................................... 20

Polar lands facts ........................... 22

Useful words ................................... 23

Find out more ................................24

Index ................................................24

# Where are the POLAR LANDS?

The coldest places on Earth are the polar regions. The Arctic is in the far north of our planet. Most of it is ocean covered in ice.

Seals live in polar regions. They feed on the fish that swim in the icy seas.

Life is hard for animals
in the polar regions because
it is so cold and dry. You can find
out about the animals that live
in the polar lands in this book.

# POLAR BEAR

Polar bears live on the Arctic ice. Their **thick** fur keeps them warm and helps them blend in with the snow and ice.

## WOW!

Polar bears have fur on the bottom of their paws.

These bears are strong swimmers. They are predators that hunt seals. A bear lies in wait at the edge of the ice. When a seal comes up for air the bear **grabs** its prey.

# HARP SEAL

Harp seals spend most of their time swimming in the Arctic Ocean. They catch fish to eat. These seals can stay underwater for 15 minutes. Sharks, polar bears and killer whales hunt them.

Baby harp seals have a fluffy white coat.

Walruses break holes in the ice with their tusks.

# WALRUS

**Huge** walruses have lots of **blubber**. This is a thick layer of fat under the skin. It keeps the animal warm. A walrus also has tusks that can be 1 m **long**.

# EMPEROR PENGUIN

The emperor penguin is the **biggest** penguin in the world. Most emperor penguins are about 110 cm tall.

The female penguin lays one egg a year. The male penguin looks after the egg until it hatches.

Emperor penguins live
in Antarctica. They have **fat**
bodies and layers of feathers.
The penguins huddle together
in big groups to keep warm.

# MUSK OX

These big, shaggy animals live in the Arctic. Their **w i d e** hooves stop them sinking into the snow.

## WOW!

A musk ox has the l o n g e s t hairs of any animal. They can be 60 cm long.

In winter, musk oxen dig through the snow to find roots, moss and lichen to eat. In summer, they eat flowers and grasses.

13

# WHALES

The blue whale is the **biggest** animal on Earth. It can grow to be 34 m long and weigh more than **180 tonnes**. Its tongue can weigh as much as an elephant!

White whales live in the Arctic Ocean. Whales live in groups called pods. They 'talk' to each other in clicks and whistles.

Blue whales swim to the polar seas in summer to find food. They eat tiny shrimp called krill.

15

# ARCTIC FOX

This fox turns white in winter. Its coat makes the fox hard to see in snow. In the summer, its coat turns brown or grey.

The Arctic fox eats lemmings, eggs and birds. This fox is jumping on a lemming under the snow.

The Arctic fox has a bushy
tail. It curls the tail around
its body when it lies down.

# LEMMING

This little animal is the size of a mouse. It has white fur in winter and brown fur in summer, like other Arctic animals.

Lemmings dig burrows to hide in. They eat plants and berries.

Arctic terns eat fish and sand eels.

# ARCTIC TERN

This bird may fly **f u r t h e r** than any bird
in the world. In the winter it lives in the Antarctic.
Then in May it flies north all the way to the
Arctic. There it makes a nest and lays eggs.

# CARIBOU

These big deer walk, or *m i g r a t e*, hundreds of kilometres north every spring. Huge herds look for grasses and plants to eat. In the summer, a caribou eats 5 to 6 kg of food a day.

A caribou's antlers can grow to 130 cm long.

As soon as snow begins to fall,
the caribou set off south again.
They may walk more than 4,900 km
every year.

# POLAR LANDS FACTS

The North Pole is the furthest north you can go on Earth. The sea ice here is 1.8 m thick.

The South Pole is the furthest south you can go. It is near the middle of the ice on Antarctica.

Icebergs are huge blocks of ice that float in the polar oceans. They can be bigger than a house!

In summer the Sun never sets near the poles. It is light all day and all night! But in winter it is dark all day.

# USEFUL WORDS

**lichen**

A living thing that grows on rocks and dead wood.

**migrate**

To move to another place. Animals migrate to find food or have young.

**predator**

An animal that hunts other animals for food. The polar bear is a predator.

**prey**

An animal hunted and eaten by another animal. Seals are the prey of a polar bear.

# FIND OUT MORE

*Animals are Amazing: Penguins,* Valerie Bodden, Franklin Watts, 2013.

*The Blue Whale,* Jenni Desmond, Enchanted Lion, 2015.

*Life Cycles: Polar Lands,* Sean Callery, Kingfisher, 2012.

*Polar Bear (A Day in the Life: Polar Animals),* Katie Marsico, Heinemann, 2011.

# INDEX

Antarctic 5, 11, 19
antlers 20
Arctic 4, 5, 6, 12, 18, 19
Arctic Ocean 8, 14

blubber 9
burrows 18

eggs 10, 16, 19

feathers 11
fur 6, 18

hooves 12

killer whales 8
krill 15

migrate 20

paws 6
pods 14
predators 7

sharks 8
snow 6, 12, 13, 16, 21
swimming 4, 7, 8, 15

tusks 9